WEST SIDE STORY

Based on a conception of Jerome Robbins

Music by
Leonard Bernstein®

Lyrics by
Stephen Sondheim

Book by
Arthur Laurents

Entire original production
directed and choreographed by

Jerome Robbins

ISBN: 978-1-61774-271-2

LEONARD
BERNSTEIN
Music Publishing
Company LLC

BOOSEY & HAWKES

AN IMAGEM COMPANY

DISTRIBUTED BY
HAL•LEONARD®
CORPORATION
7777 W. BLUEMOUND RD. P.O. BOX 13819 MILWAUKEE, WI 53213

www.leonardbernstein.com
www.boosey.com
www.halleonard.com

CONTENTS

SOMETHING'S COMING

Lyrics by STEPHEN SONDHEIM
Music by LEONARD BERNSTEIN
Arranged by Carol Klose

CHA-CHA FROM THE DANCE AT THE GYM

Lyrics by STEPHEN SONDHEIM
Music by LEONARD BERNSTEIN
Arranged by Carol Klose

MARIA

Lyrics by STEPHEN SONDHEIM
Music by LEONARD BERNSTEIN
Arranged by Carol Klose

TONIGHT

Lyrics by STEPHEN SONDHEIM
Music by LEONARD BERNSTEIN
Arranged by Carol Klose

Steady Latin beat

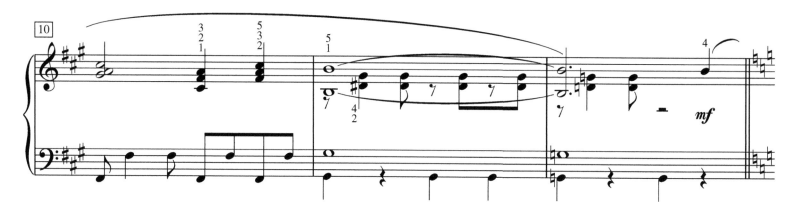

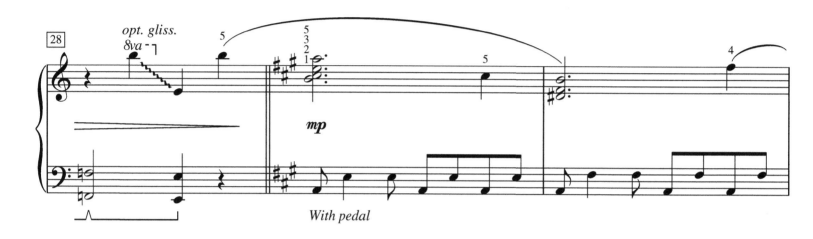

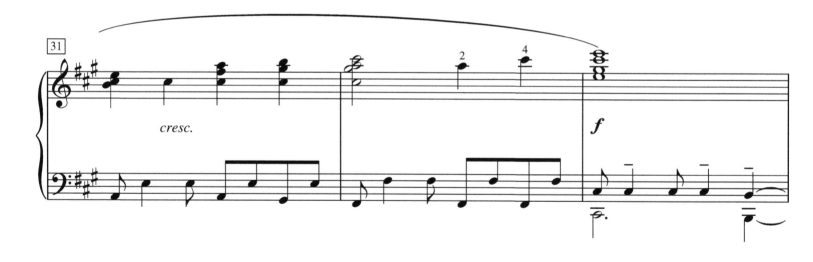

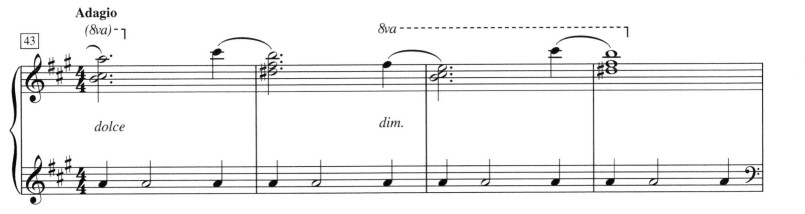

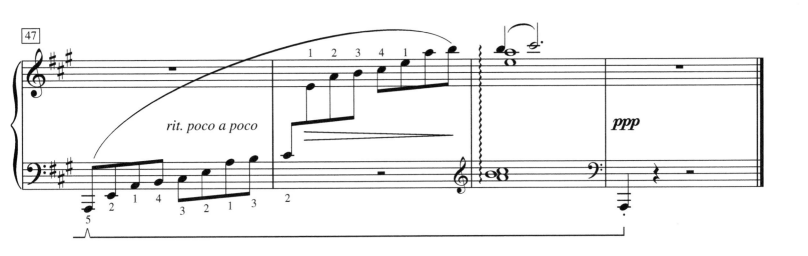

AMERICA

Lyrics by STEPHEN SONDHEIM
Music by LEONARD BERNSTEIN
Arranged by Carol Klose

Brightly, with a strong beat

COOL

Lyrics by STEPHEN SONDHEIM
Music by LEONARD BERNSTEIN
Arranged by Carol Klose

ONE HAND, ONE HEART

Lyrics by STEPHEN SONDHEIM
Music by LEONARD BERNSTEIN
Arranged by Carol Klose

I FEEL PRETTY

Lyrics by STEPHEN SONDHEIM
Music by LEONARD BERNSTEIN
Arranged by Carol Klose

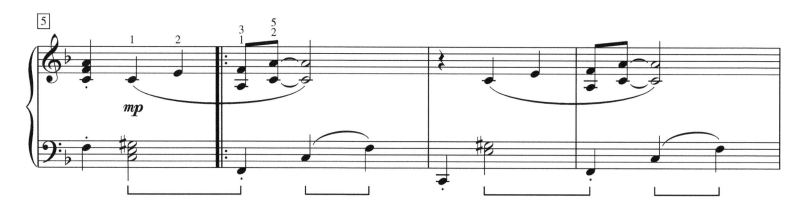

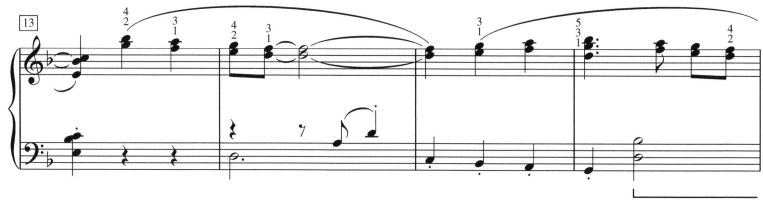

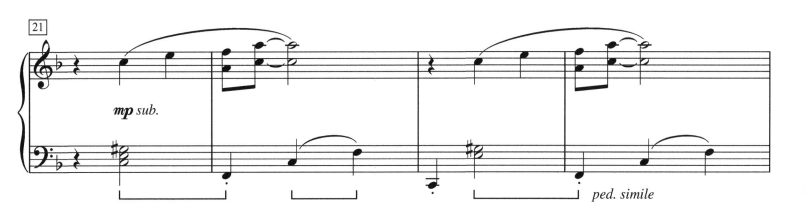

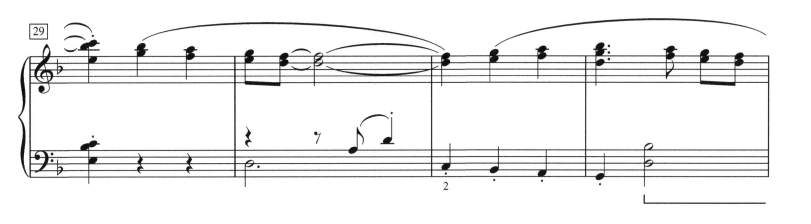

SOMEWHERE

Lyrics by STEPHEN SONDHEIM
Music by LEONARD BERNSTEIN
Arranged by Carol Klose

Slowly, with reverence

ppp

pp legato

With pedal (opt. una corda pedal)

poco cresc.

mp

flowing and expressive

(tre corde)

simile

cresc.

Poco più mosso

Tempo I

I HAVE A LOVE

Lyrics by STEPHEN SONDHEIM
Music by LEONARD BERNSTEIN
Arranged by Carol Klose

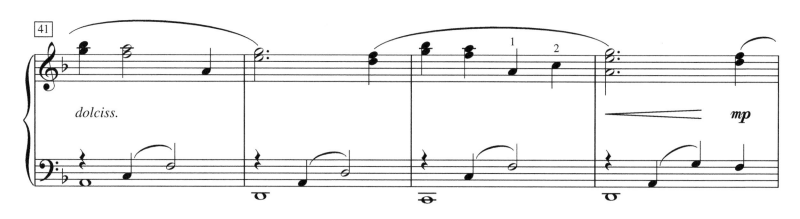

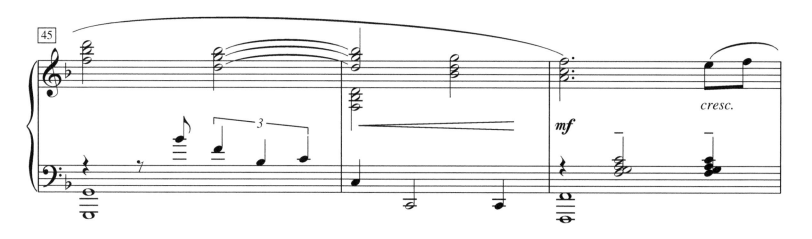

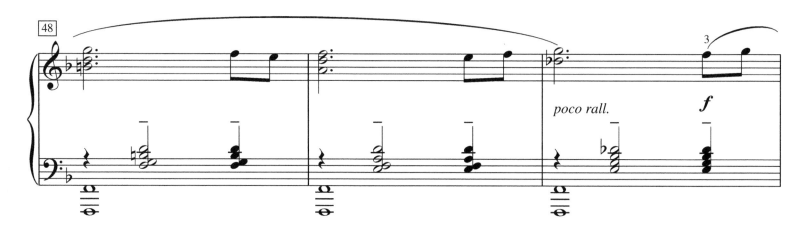

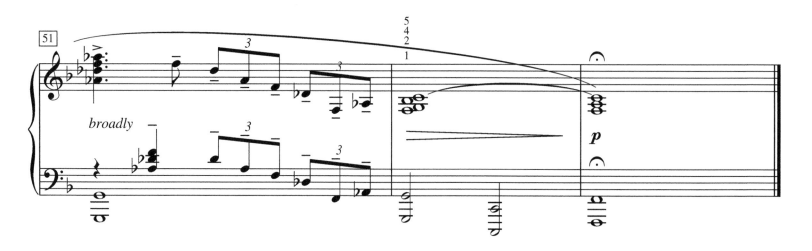